PEACEFUL PROSPERITY

TAKING THE FEAR OUT OF FINANCE

Workbook

Lotus Tribe Studios

Austin, Texas

Edited by Anna Jaworski / Baby Hearts Press and Amy M. Le / Quill Hawk Publishing
Cover Design by Omer Farooq

Workbook Design by Jenny Muscatell
Images used with permission via Canva Pro licensing agreement
ISBN (paperback): 978-1-960932-00-6
ISBN (e-book): 978-1-960932-01-3

PEACEFUL PROSPERITY

TAKING THE FEAR OUT OF FINANCE

What Others Are Saying About the Workshops:

"A fresh perspective on a rather dry and vulnerable topic. The revealing exercises helped me understand the underlying behavior driving my financial decisions. I appreciated the reframing." -LS

"Amazing, beneficial, surprising, and at its heart, not as much about money as it is about expanding our minds, exploring our potential, and getting concrete evidence immediately that we are better as a group than we are alone." -AS

"A foundational look at personal finance and how your beliefs about money can affect how you feel, what you do, and ultimately your overall financial health. The exercises are concrete work that gave me ideas for what to focus on next. This made it easy to see how it all fits together." -AP

"Finance in language I could understand, hallelujah!" -DG

Acknowledgements

To Kyle Mitchell for his "check-ins" concept.

To Barbara Huson for her kindness in sharing the Roots Exercise.

To Lisa Feder for her co-creation of the mindful meditations.

To Amy Samet for her help in crafting the Transferable Skills Exercise.

To Karen McCall for her kindness in sharing the Discover Your Earnings Ceiling Exercise.

To Bari Tessler for her inspiration behind Renaming My Monthly Expenses and the Money Date.

To Anna Jaworski for her idea for the Credit Score Scavenger Hunt.

To Ryan Redfern for his insight in creating the Balance Sheet Observations.

To Susan Bradley for her generosity in sharing the Communication Preferences sheet.

To Jenny Muscatell for her talent and dedication in making this all come together so beautifully.

To all of the women who have attended the workshops, provided honest feedback, and encouraged me to never stop improving.

Thank you so much for your invaluable contributions!

-Laura-

Contents

HOW TO USE THIS WORKBOOK

Welcome to YOUR space! This workbook was created just for you, as a place to practice what you learn as you make your way through the concepts of the Peaceful Prosperity series.

This workbook is a companion to the first *Peaceful Prosperity* book, *Taking the Fear Out of Finance.*

Taking the Fear Out of Finance is a journey up your financial mountain. We start at Base Camp, establishing your foundation. Then we climb upwards, helping you create and practice useful financial habits. Finally, we arrive at the summit, where you will expand your vision and open your financial world to even greater possibilities.

Along the way, we consider you as a whole person and look at more than the money you have in the bank. We consider your financial well-being from multiple vantage points. We'll also take mental breaks periodically, to stop, reflect, and process the journey.

By the end of Book One, you will have covered all the basics, gaining the confidence and skills to establish Peaceful Prosperity in your life.

BASE CAMP CHECK-IN

Is there a word, phrase, or quote that describes where you are now? Write it here.

You Are Here

Money Date

Balance Sheet

Credit + Debt

Expenses

Income

Money Mindset

"A lack of knowledge creates fear. Seeking knowledge creates courage."– Candice Swanepoel

What epiphanies or "Aha" moments have you experienced so far?

What are your questions?

What are your fears?

What do you hope to learn or accomplish?

Chapter One

Money Mindset

Digging Down to the Roots Exercise

*From *Overcoming Underearning* by Barbara Stanny

Complete the following sentences with the first words that come to mind. Don't censure what you get or look for the "right" answer. Let yourself go with your very first reaction. And do it quickly. You can always change your responses later.

1   My biggest fear about money is

....

2   My father felt money was

....

3   My mother felt money was

....

4   In my family, money caused

....

5   My early experience with money was

....

6 Money equals

....

7 I'm afraid if I had more money, I would

....

8 In order to have more money, I'd need to

....

9 When I have money, I usually

....

10 If I could afford it, I would

....

11 People with money are

....

12 I'd have more money if

....

What did you learn?

....

....

....

How did your early experiences and parental messages affect you?

....

....

What would you like to change?

....

....

Discuss your responses with at least one other person. Continue to mull them over for the next few days and see what comes up for you.

....

....

....

....

Peaceful Prosperity Notes

Bonus Visualization Exercise
Money Mindset

Take a moment to look again at what you wrote for the first answer of the "Digging Down to the Roots" exercise. If you can, allow yourself to sit with your fears about money. Take a moment to absorb the words you wrote. No need to change them; just observe.

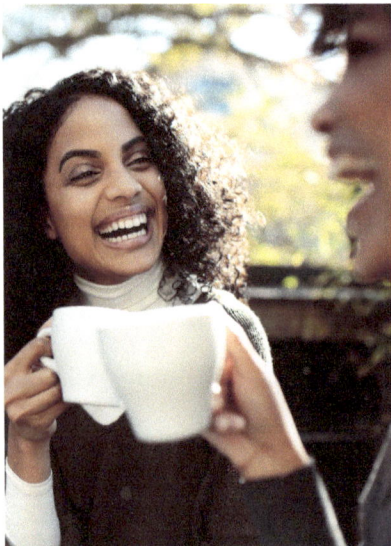

Now close your eyes and imagine your best friend. Bring to mind your friend's face, voice, and smile. Imagine your friend is sitting with you right now. Your friend tells you that they are feeling these emotions and fears about money.

What would you say? How would you counsel your friend?

....

....

....

"The compassionate path is far, far more effective in creating sustainable transformation than the self-critical one." – Bari Tessler

What would you say?

Do you notice any strengths that your friend already possesses that can help overcome this fear? Is your friend forgetting about some skills and talents that could help in this situation? Have similar challenges been overcome in the past? What would you say to point this out?

....

....

....

Take a deep breath.

Now, picture hugging your friend and letting go of the image. Take a deep breath.

Can you say the same words of encouragement to yourself? Give it a try.

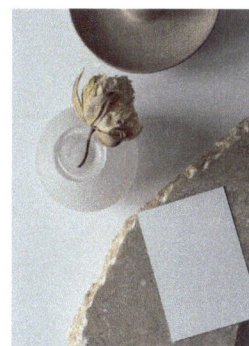

Thank yourself.

Take another breath and thank yourself for being truly brave and facing your fears today. You're doing great! Hug yourself before returning to your day.

YOUR ASCENT CHECK-IN

Is there a word, phrase, or quote that describes where you are now? Write it here.

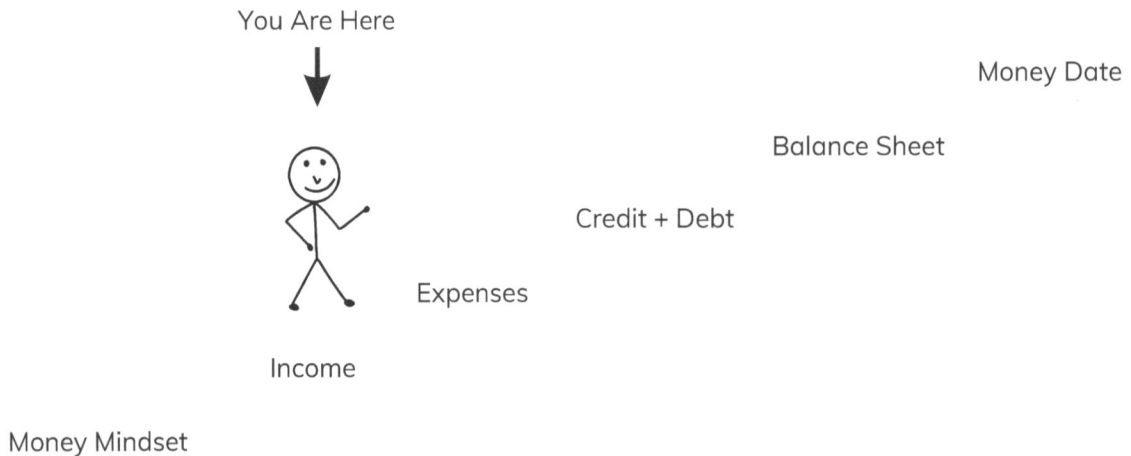

You Are Here

Money Date

Balance Sheet

Credit + Debt

Expenses

Income

Money Mindset

> If knowledge is power, then curiosity is the muscle. –
> Danielle LaPorte

What epiphanies or "Aha" moments have you experienced so far?

What are your questions?

What are your fears?

What do you hope to learn or accomplish?

Peaceful Prosperity Notes

Chapter Two

The Invisible Column: Income

EXPANDING YOUR INCOME

"If you don't like the road you're walking, start paving another one. – Dolly Parton

1. My Current Monthly Income:

Description	Frequency (Weekly, Monthly, Quarterly)	Current Amount	Desired Amount
Wages / Paycheck			
Investments			
Real Estate / Rental Income			
Royalties			
Self-employment / Side Hustle			
TOTAL			

Go to peaceful-prosperity.com/workbookdownloads for an easy-to-use electronic format.

EXPANDING YOUR INCOME

What goals would you be setting for
yourself if you knew you could not fail?
- Robert H. Schuller

2. Side Hustle Ideas to Consider:

Name/ Activity	Requirements to Start	Training, Supplies, Equipment	Expected Earnings	Expected Hours	Expected Expenses	Mentors to Ask

Go to peaceful-prosperity.com/workbookdownloads for an easy-to-use electronic format.

EXPANDING YOUR INCOME

" We are not victims of our situation. We are the architects of it. -Simon Sinek

3. How else can I increase / expand my income?

Transferable Skills Exercise

"You are far too smart to be the only thing standing in your way."

-Jennifer J Freeman

Something I've done that I am proud of:

....

....

....

Three traits/skills that helped me achieve that:

1. ....

2. ....

3. ....

Transferable Skills Exercise

Something I'm currently struggling with financially:

What have I tried so far to ease the struggle or improve the situation?

What else could I try?

Go back to the traits/skills you listed. How could those traits/skills help with your current struggle?

What will I try next? When?

Peaceful Prosperity Notes

*Discover Your Earnings Ceiling**
**Created by Karen McCall, Founder of the Financial Recovery Institute*

Get comfortable, relax your whole body, and picture yourself in a lovely, calm, serene setting. When you're ready, read the first line, then close your eyes and consider your answer. After a few seconds of meditation, open your eyes and write your response. Then read the next line and repeat.

1. Imagine you are earning $5,000 a year. How do you feel? What are your thoughts?

2. Imagine you are earning $10,000 a year. How do you feel? What are your thoughts?

3. Imagine you are earning $25,000 a year. How do you feel? What are your thoughts?

Discover Your Earnings Ceiling*
*Created by Karen McCall, Founder of the Financial Recovery Institute

4. Imagine you are earning $50,000 a year. How do you feel? What are your thoughts?

5. Imagine you are earning $75,000 a year. How do you feel? What are your thoughts?

6. Imagine you are earning $100,000 a year. How do you feel? What are your thoughts?

*Discover Your Earnings Ceiling**
**Created by Karen McCall, Founder of the Financial Recovery Institute*

7. Imagine you are earning $250,000 a year. How do you feel? What are your thoughts?

8. Imagine you are earning $500,000 a year. How do you feel? What are your thoughts?

9. Imagine you are earning $1,000,000 a year. How do you feel? What are your thoughts?

10. What did you discover? Were there any surprises? How high was your ceiling? What does this tell you?

....

....

Chapter Three

The Troublesome Column: Expenses

PEACEFUL PROSPERITY
My Monthly Expenses

Current Name	New Name	Amount (Guess)	Amount (Actual)
Federal Income Taxes (Payroll) (SS, FICA, Medicare)			
401(k)/IRA/Retirement Savings			
Other Savings Account(s)			
Rent/Mortgage Payment			
Property Taxes			
HOA Dues			
Utilities: Electric, Gas, Sewer/Water			
Cable/Internet			
Phone			
Groceries			
Eating Out			
Entertainment			
Credit Card Payment(s)			
Student Loan Payment(s)			
Car Payment/Transportation			
Gas/Car Maintenance			
Car Insurance			

PEACEFUL PROSPERITY
My Monthly Expenses

Current Name	New Name	Amount (Guess)	Amount (Actual)
Health Insurance			
Life Insurance			
Home/Renters Insurance			
Medical (prescriptions, copays)			
Child Care			
Child Support/Alimony			
Pets			
Charity/Church			
Gifts			
Recreation/Travel			
Clothing/Hair			
Self Care			
Other			

Go to peaceful-prosperity.com/workbookdownloads for an easy-to-use electronic format.

What Am I Saving For?

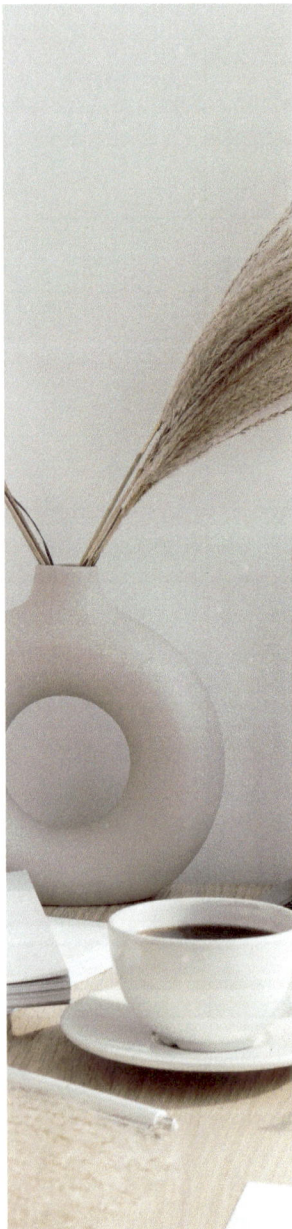

"Courage is created by seeing the good."
— *Meir Ezra*

Saving money gets easier when you have a powerful reason to help motivate you through the tough stuff. What's your powerful reason to save money?

....

....

....

Do you want to travel? Improve your home? Help a child? Buy something special? The next page is space for you to dream. You can use words, pictures, cartoon scribbles... whatever helps you to envision your reasons and the results you desire from saving money. Go ahead.

Peaceful Prosperity Notes

Chapter Four

The Double-Edged Sword: Credit & Debt

PEACEFUL PROSPERITY
Credit Score Scavenger Hunt

I would like my Credit Score to be: By This Date:

Because:

Date	Credit Score	Source	Next Step
01/01/2023	700	TransUnion	Ask for an increase in credit limit on Mastercard

Date I Reached My Credit Score Goal: Score:

PEACEFUL PROSPERITY
Credit Score Scavenger Hunt

What will I do to celebrate when I have reached my credit score goal?

What will I do to keep my score high?

Debt Description
Part One

1. When I hear the word DEBT, I think of:

2. These are the words I use to describe DEBT:

3. These are the images I picture when I think about DEBT:

"Prosperity is a way of living and thinking, and not just money or things. Poverty is a way of living and thinking, and not just a lack of money or things."

–ERIC BUTTERWORTH

4. This is how it makes me feel:

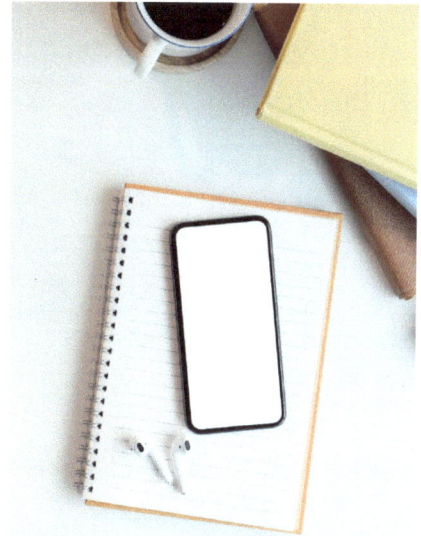

Debt Description
Part Two

1. When I step back from my debt, I observe that:

2. What words could I use instead?

3. How do these new words make me feel?

Bonus Challenge
Personifying Debt

1 If my debt were a person or an animal, it would look like...

....

2 It would sound like....

....

....

3 It would smell like...

....

....

4 Here's how I can turn my debt into something ridiculous

that makes me laugh:

....

....

....

5 What else can I do to feel like I have I have power

over my debt?

....

....

....

Debt Reduction Worksheet

1. Example

What	Creditor	Balance	Rate	Minimum Due	Monthly Payment
Home Mortgage	Chase Bank	$188,000	4.50%	$605	$605
Citibank Mastercard	Citibank	$4,986	19.99%	$100	$100
Honda CRV	Honda	$11,400	2.99%	$400	$400
Student Loan	Navient	$20,000	4.60%	$300	$350
Lowe's Credit Card	Chase Bank	$250	24.99%	$50	$50
TOTAL DEBT		**$224,636**		**$1,455**	**$1,700**

2. Your Turn

What	Creditor	Balance	Rate	Minimum Due	Monthly Payment
TOTAL DEBT		**$0**		**$0**	**$0**

Go to peaceful-prosperity.com/workbookdownloads for an easy-to-use electronic format.

Relax and Integrate
Meditation

The purpose of this meditation is to absorb any new information; recognize the amazing work you are doing; and praise yourself for how far you have come on this journey. The experience should feel like a reward. Sit for a moment and savor any successes or epiphanies you have experienced so far.

Meditations don't require you to close your eyes, although you certainly can.

Meditations don't require you to SAY anything special; however, you might want to consider creating your own personal, financial mantra or affirmation and say that to yourself.

Meditations don't require you to sit cross-legged, either, although you certainly can. You can meditate in any position: sitting, standing, walking, or lying down.

For this meditation, take a moment to focus on your breath flowing in and out. Feel the comforting power of your breath, always present, always supporting you.

Take a moment to scan your body and identify any areas that feel tense. Imagine the warm sun gently shining on those areas, inviting them to relax and open.

Next, bring to mind your financial goal, and begin to picture all the tools you now have to help you with that goal.

These could be a concept you learned, a number you discovered, or an activity you experienced.

....

....

....

Say to yourself: "I am strong. I am educating myself. I've got this! I am taking the fear out of finance. I will experience Peaceful Prosperity."

"To experience peace does not mean that your life is always blissful. It means that you are capable of tapping into a blissful state of mind amidst the normal chaos of a hectic life."
-Jill Bolte Taylor

My Ideal Life Exercise

Imagine you are living your ideal life. Take a moment to visualize it in every detail. Breathe in deeply and look around your ideal life. Describe it as if it is happening right now.

1 Where am I?

....

....

What does it LOOK like?

....

....

What does it FEEL like?

....

....

What does it SOUND like?

....

....

2 Who am I with?

....

....

....

My Ideal Life Exercise

3   What am I doing?

....

....

....

4   What's my normal routine?

....

....

....

5   Who am I being?

....

....

....

6   What makes me feel pleased and proud of myself?

....

....

....

My Ideal Life Exercise

7   I want this vision because...

....

....

....

8   In pursuit of this, the largest obstacles might be...

....

....

....

9   I will overcome these obstacles by...

....

....

....

"Today's accomplishments were yesterday's impossibilities."
-Robert Schuller

Peaceful Prosperity Notes

THE SUMMIT CHECK-IN

Is there a word, phrase, or quote that describes where you are now? Write it here.

You Are Here

↓

Money Date

Balance Sheet

Credit + Debt

Expenses

Income

Money Mindset

"Each fresh peak ascended teaches something."
– Sir Martin Convey

What epiphanies or "Aha" moments have you experienced so far?

What are your questions?

What are your fears?

What do you hope to learn or accomplish?

Chapter Five

Balance Sheet Discoveries

My Balance Sheet

Year:	Example	2023	2024	2025
Assets				
Checking Account 1	$100			
Checking Account 2	$5,000			
CDs/Money Market	$10,000			
Savings Account 1	$200			
Savings Account 2	$500			
Savings Account 3	$5,000			
Employer Plan/401(k)	$25,050			
IRA	$7,012			
Roth IRA	$15,233			
Cash Value Life Insurance	$0			
Other Investments	$0			
Primary Residence	$300,000			
Other Real Estate	$0			
Vehicle 1	$2,500			
Vehicle 2	$5,500			
Jewelry/Collectibles	$0			
Other	$0			
Total Assets	**$376,095**			

Go to peaceful-prosperity.com/workbookdownloads for an easy-to-use electronic format.

My Balance Sheet

Year:	Example	2023	2024	2025
Liabilities				
Mortgage	$222,035			
HELOC	$0			
Student Loan	$23,000			
Vehicle Loan 1	$0			
Vehicle Loan 2	$15,000			
Credit Card 1	$12,000			
Credit Card 2	$600			
Outstanding Medical Bills	$0			
Other Debt	$0			
Total Liabilities	**$272,635**			
Grand Total (Assets - Liabilities)	**$103,460**			
Change From Prior Year				

Go to peaceful-prosperity.com/workbookdownloads for an easy-to-use electronic format.

Peaceful Prosperity - Workbook 45

Peaceful Prosperity Notes

Balance Sheet Observations

Date:

Take a deep breath. Let it go. Applaud yourself for having done the work on your balance sheet. Now let's harvest those lessons!

What were your 2-3 biggest wins or accomplishments this year?

What were your 2-3 biggest strengths? (This doesn't have to be the same as your "wins.")

What worked this year? Why?

BALANCE SHEET OBSERVATIONS

What didn't work so well this year? Why?

What were your 2-3 biggest setbacks or challenges this year?

What were your 2-3 greatest weaknesses? (This doesn't have to be the same as your "setbacks.")

BALANCE SHEET OBSERVATIONS

How far did you get on your goals? If it's helpful, you could give yourself a scale.

For example: Rate yourself a "1" if you didn't work on the goal at all, a "5" if you reached the goal, and a "3" for someplace in between. Or you can write a narrative instead. Use whatever feels most helpful to you. There is an example below.

Sample Goal	Paying off Car
How far did I get?	*I only have 2 more payments!*

Goal One	
How far did I get?	

Goal Two	
How far did I get?	

BALANCE SHEET OBSERVATIONS

Now let's think about the coming year.

What are 2-3 things you want to *continue* doing?

What are 2-3 things you want to stop doing?

What are 2-3 new things you want to *start* doing?

"It is often the small steps, not the giant leaps, that bring about the most lasting change." - Queen Elizabeth II of England

Chapter Six

The Art of the Money Date and Better Money Conversations

Money Date Exercise

MY MONEY DATE

"I feel myself becoming the fearless person I have dreamt of being. Have I arrived? No. But I'm constantly evolving and challenging myself to be unafraid to make mistakes." -Janelle Monae

When I take myself on a Money Date, I will find a comfortable place. I will lovingly bring the following:

Hearing: (favorite song)

Taste: (favorite treat)

Smell: (candle or perfume)

Touch: (favorite pen or paper)

Sight: (photo or screensaver)

I will take myself on a Money Date (i.e., monthly or when I get paid):

....

....

....

On today's Money Date I plan to accomplish:

....

....

....

I will take a deep breath and

give myself a hug before I begin.

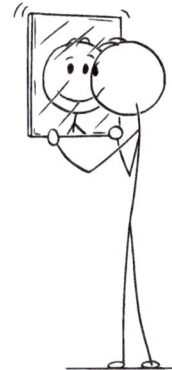

On today's Money Date I did accomplish:

....

....

....

My next Money Date is:

....

COMMUNICATION PREFERENCES
Exercise

Personal finance is a very private topic, one we usually do not share with many people. Because it is private, it is also an infrequent topic and we do not get many opportunities to discover how to have comfortable and productive money conversations. We all have a preferred style of communicating when we are talking about our money and key commitments.

Finance-related discussions are more productive and less volatile when we know one another's communication styles.
The following exercise is designed to allow you to quickly identify your primary communication preferences when talking about money with your partner / spouse.

COMMUNICATION PREFERENCES
Exercise

Select the top three sentences that best describe how you prefer to discuss financial topics.

_ Encourage my input.	_ Encourage my input.
_ Be an active listener.	_ Be an active listener.
_ Remember my need for control.	_ Remember my need for control.
_ Give direct answers; get to the point.	_ Give direct answers; get to the point.
_ Move quickly to the bottom line.	_ Move quickly to the bottom line.
_ Offer options so I can decide.	_ Offer options so I can decide.
_ Allow me time to process my response.	_ Allow me time to process my response.
_ Tell me who is involved.	_ Tell me who is involved.
_ Use logic, summaries, and key points.	_ Use logic, summaries, and key points.

When we talk about money, please remember my tendency to:

....

and my need for:

....

Now that you have identified your preferences, discuss these together to understand how each of you can help both people feel comfortable and productive in financial discussions. How do you like to receive information and recommendations? How can you support each other when decisions need to be made? Write down your expectations and agreements on the next page to help you both remember how you can work together as a team. Keep in mind that these statements can change over time. Agree to revisit this topic every so often.

COMMUNICATION PREFERENCES

Agreements

1   In a romantic partnership, I expect myself to:

....

....

2   I expect my spouse/partner to:

....

....

3   How large purchase decisions will be made:

....

....

4   How long-term investment decisions will be made:

....

....

COMMUNICATION PREFERENCES

Considerations

Feeling Disconnected

If you are ever disconnected, not feeling good about a meeting or discussion we are having, what would I see? If I think I see that behavior, is it okay if I check in with you?

Taking A Break

If you need to take a break from discussions and/or decision making, would you let me know? Sometimes money discussions can be exhausting. Together we can easily structure a time-out that will give you the peace of mind that you need. When we do this, let's agree to come back together and continue the conversation in a specific amount of time, so we're both comfortable with the pause.

We will revisit this conversation:

"FEELING RICH" MEDITATION

"Abundance and prosperity begin with gratitude and appreciation." – Anthon St. Maarten

Find a quiet spot where you can relax without distractions for a few minutes. Get comfortable wherever you are. Take a deep breath, then let it out with a sigh.

Breathe normally and focus on your breath flowing in and out for a couple of breath cycles. Feel the comforting power of your breath, always present, always supporting you.

Relax your shoulders. Relax your hands. Relax your jaw. Imagine the warm sun gently shining on your body, inviting any areas of tension to relax and open.

"Feeling Rich" Meditation

Next, bring to mind a time when you felt "rich," "abundant," or "blessed" in your life. Where were you? Who were you with? What was happening?

Why did you feel joyful at this moment? What words would you use to describe the feeling?

As you remember this feeling, notice how it feels in your body. Is there anywhere you feel a pleasant sensation? Perhaps you feel warmth in your heart. Or perhaps there's a tingle in your fingers. Or expansion in your belly. See if you can connect with that sensation, and savor it for a moment.

"Feeling Rich" Meditation

Say to yourself, "I am here. I have arrived. Whatever I may have gone through in the past, I am here now. I feel good. I feel prosperous. I feel happy." (Use your own words to describe the positive feelings you experienced in this memory.)

End the meditation with: "I am here. This is what it is like to experience Peaceful Prosperity."

———————

"You keep putting one foot in front of the other, and then one day you look back and you've climbed a mountain." – Tom Hiddleston

CONCLUSION CHECK-IN

Is there a word, phrase, or quote that describes where you are now? Write it here.

What's Next?

Money Date

Balance Sheet

Credit + Debt

Expenses

Income

Money Mindset

> "Climb mountains not so the world can see you, but so you can see the world." – David McCullough Jr.

What epiphanies or "Aha" moments have you experienced on this journey?

Look back at your previous three check-in's. What has changed?

What can you be proud of or celebrate?

What do you want to learn or do next?

Would you like to continue taking the fear out of finance? Visit the Peaceful Prosperity website for more!
peaceful-prosperity.com

WORKSHOPS and ONE-ON-ONE COACHING

Engage with other money adventurers in an intimate small group setting, or engage with me one-on-one. We discuss the concepts in the book and explore your own personal money story. I answer your questions and help you find solutions to your financial challenges. Visit the website for availability and dates.

BOOK TWO: CREATING YOUR FINANCIAL FUTURE

My next book, *Peaceful Prosperity: Creating Your Financial Future* will be coming out soon. You can look on Amazon, or better yet, sign up for the newsletter to receive updates.

NEWSLETTER

Sign up at peaceful-prosperity.com to receive monthly tips, affirmations, and fresh ideas. Subscribers also get updates on new books and access to new offerings before they are available to the public!

YOUTUBE

Go to peaceful-prosperity.com and click on "Resources" to access free videos I record and post periodically, full of encouragement and insights.

About the Author

Laura Redfern, CFP®, CeFT® is a financial planner, writer, coach, and creator of the *Peaceful Prosperity* Workshops, a series of financial education classes for women.

Laura fell into finance unexpectedly, after studying education, theatre, and British Literature at Capital University in Columbus, Ohio. A natural teacher, Laura has helped guide hundreds of individuals and couples to a better relationship with their money over the past 20 years.

Laura now lives in Austin, Texas with her husband Ryan. When she's not working, she's likely to be found drinking tea, eating tacos, or binge-watching Disney movies.

References

All materials referencing Barbara Stanny used with permission by Barbara Huson, formerly Barbara Stanny. www.barbara-huson.com

"Digging Down to the Roots" exercise from the book Overcoming Underearning™. Copyright © 2005 by Barbara Stanny.

All materials referencing Karen McCall used with permission by Karen McCall. www.moneygrit.com.

"Discover Your Earnings Ceiling" from the book Financial Recovery. Copyright © 2011 by Karen McCall. Reprinted with permission of New World Library, Novato, CA. www.newworldlibrary.com

All materials referencing Susan Bradley used with permission by Susan Bradley. www.suddenmoney.com

"Communication Preferences" exercise modified and used with permission from Susan Bradley. Copyright © 2019 Yeldarb Properties, LLC.

PEACEFUL PROSPERITY
TAKING THE FEAR OUT OF FINANCE